Dive to the Deep Ocean

Voyages of Exploration and Discovery

Deborah Kovacs

RSVP

**RAINTREE
STECK-VAUGHN**

P U B L I S H E R S
A Steck-Vaughn Company

Austin, Texas

www.steck-vaughn.com

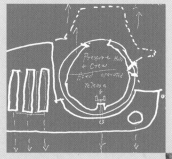

In Memory of Allyn Vine (1915-1994),
Maverick

Steck-Vaughn Company

First published 2000 by Raintree Steck-Vaughn Publishers,
an imprint of Steck-Vaughn Company.

Library of Congress Cataloging-in-Publication Data
Kovacs, Deborah.
    Dive to the deep ocean: voyages of exploration and discovery / Deborah Kovacs.
      p.   cm. — (Turnstone ocean explorer book)
    Includes bibliographical references and index.
    Summary: Relates the history of deep sea research, explaining how the development of
    submersibles, particularly the Alvin, has led to many fascinating discoveries.
    ISBN 0-7398-1234-3 hb. — ISBN 0-7398-1235-1 sb
    1. Underwater exploration — Juvenile literature.   2. Oceanographic submersibles — Juvenile
literature. [1. Underwater exploration. 2.Oceanographic submersibles. 3. Alvin (Submarine)]
I. Title.   II. Series.
GC65.K68   1999
623.8'205 — dc21   99-17877
                                      CIP

For information about this and other Turnstone
reference books and educational materials, visit
Turnstone Publishing Group on the World Wide
Web at http://www.turnstonepub.com.

Printed and bound in the United States of America

1 2 3 4 5 6 7 8 9 0 LB 04 03 02 01 00 99

CONTENTS

1

DREAMING OF THE DEEP

"I think that a lot of oceanographers wish they had been born a century ago or two centuries ago, because they are explorers at heart. If they were born a century ago, they would be out exploring some canyon in the west that nobody had seen before. Now, since those canyons have all been explored, they get in submersibles."
—Oceanographer Lauren Mullineaux

Fighting the rough seas of the North Atlantic on a windy summer day in 1938, scientists and crew aboard the research vessel *Atlantis* leaned hard to turn the heavy handle of a winch. Attached to the winch were hundreds of feet of rope running down to a large net. With each turn of the handle, the net was pulled closer to the surface. Finally the net cleared the waves. Huge, dripping, and loaded with creatures, it was hauled onto the deck.

Most of the animals were dead or mangled. Even so, to many of the scientists on board, the net held fascinating clues to the mysterious, unknown ocean. They quickly went to work, identifying each animal, placing those still alive in buckets of saltwater, and putting dead creatures into containers of preservative for later study.

One young man stood thoughtfully at the edge of the group, eyeing the mass of squashed animals. Allyn Vine was a graduate student spending the summer on Cape Cod, Massachusetts, as a researcher at the new Woods Hole Oceanographic Institution (or WHOI, pronounced "HOO-ee"). Allyn loved to solve problems, and here was one staring him in the face. Was *this* the best way to understand life in the deep ocean? Wouldn't biologists learn a lot more about these animals by traveling down

(above)
Researchers haul sampling nets onto the decks of Atlantis.

(left inset)
Allyn Vine (left) and his advisor, Dr. Maurice Ewing, get ready to test an underwater camera in 1940.

(left)
Most open-ocean research at WHOI from 1931 to 1963 was done aboard Atlantis.

5

According to legend, Greek king Alexander the Great was lowered underwater in a glass box as long ago as 330 B.C.

Robert Fulton's submersible, Nautilus, was designed to be operated by two people. One turned a crank to operate the sub's propellor, and the other person steered.

into their world, to see where they came from? To Allyn, trying to understand the world of the deep sea by sending down nets was like reaching blindfolded into a big bag. It was impossible for the scientists to know what they would pull out—or what they might have missed.

Allyn's imagination started working on the problem. What about an underwater camera towed from a ship? Or nets that could open and shut at different depths? These were good ideas, and he soon began creating these tools.

But another dream, much bigger than the others and way ahead of its time, began to occupy Allyn. What about a vehicle to carry people to the deepest parts of the ocean where they could see what was there, move around, and even collect samples?

This wasn't an entirely new idea. The notion of traveling down into the ocean has been around at least since the time of Alexander the Great (356–323 B.C.). Since then, famous inventors have explored this possibility. In the fifteenth century Leonardo da Vinci drew several different submersible designs. Nineteenth-century steamship inventor Robert Fulton built *Nautilus*, the first multiple-passenger submersible.

Submarines were being used in 1938 when Allyn Vine began studying the problem of submersibles. But

they were almost all built as weapons, and rarely traveled deeper than a few hundred meters.

There was even a research sub at that time. Called a bathysphere, it had taken its inventors, William Beebe and Otis Barton, to a depth of 922 meters (3,028 feet). But the bathysphere had limitations. Its windows were barely the size of a person's face. And because it was attached to the surface by a heavy cable, it could only travel straight down and up, like an underwater elevator. It was dangerous, too.

Allyn wondered if there were better ways to explore the deep. The bathysphere's windows were tiny. Would it be possible to sink down inside a glass ball? He asked engineers at the Corning Glass Factory in New York in 1939. They listened with interest to his idea, but told him it was not practical.

So Allyn Vine put aside his idea about traveling down into the deep ocean for a while, but he kept the idea in the back of his mind. As he worked with submarines during World War II, Allyn kept wishing they had windows so he could see what was going on under the water's surface. When the war ended, he began to talk more and more about this hope, and to write letters to anybody he thought could help make this happen.

Surprisingly, the very hardest group to convince was fellow ocean scientists. "Too risky," he was told, over and over again. "It's too expensive. It's too uncertain." And besides, most people thought that the deep seafloor was a lifeless desert. So why bother to go there?

Deep-sea explorer William Beebe sits perched atop his bathysphere, a water-tight, deep-sea "elevator" with small crystal windows. In the 1930s, the bathysphere carried people to depths never reached before.

Why go there? That was the one question Allyn just wouldn't accept. He thought the seafloor probably had as many amazing sights as the most spectacular places on dry land. "The deep ocean was…where our gang expected to find the most fun, and the most answers," he said. New worlds surely lay in the depths.

Over time, more and more people began to see the importance of traveling to the deep ocean. In the 1950s, two Frenchmen, August Picard and his son, Jacques, built an experimental sub called *Trieste,* which the U.S. Navy bought in 1958. Though much larger and deeper-diving than Beebe and Otis' bathysphere, it, too, was little more than an underwater elevator.

Still, on January 23, 1960, this "elevator" managed to reach the very bottom of the Marianas Trench, a 10,900-meter (35,800-foot) slash in the seafloor that is the deepest part of the ocean. Though that is an impressive achievement that has yet to be repeated, the *Trieste* divers, Jacques Picard and Navy Lieutenant Don Walsh, didn't see much more than mud and a startled rat-tail fish on their trip. But though it could dive deeply, *Trieste* was huge, and it could only travel straight up and down.

The seafloor is not flat. Like dry land, it is full of features, such as mountains, volcanoes, valleys, and even deep slashes, which are called trenches.

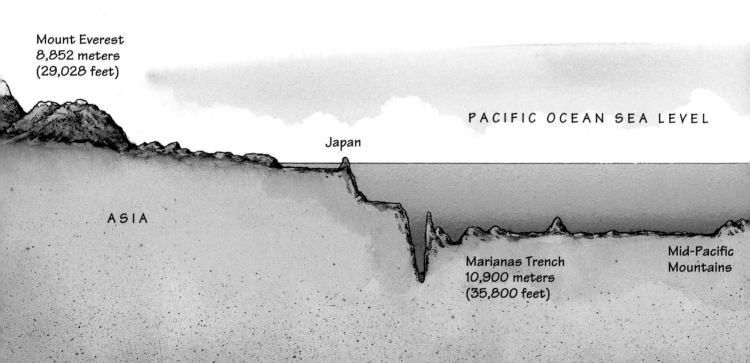

Mount Everest
8,852 meters
(29,028 feet)

PACIFIC OCEAN SEA LEVEL

Japan

ASIA

Marianas Trench
10,900 meters
(35,800 feet)

Mid-Pacific
Mountains

Allyn and others wanted a submersible that could move around under battery power and that was small enough to be easily carried out to sea.

Finally, in 1962, at about the same time that astronauts first began to travel in outer space, Charles "Swede" Momsen made an important decision. Chief of Undersea Warfare at the Navy's Office for Naval Research, he decided it was time for the U.S. Navy to fund the construction of a submersible that was smaller and more maneuverable than any that had yet been built. While Swede knew that the new sub would be very useful to scientists, he also knew that the Navy could use it to do deep-ocean rescue work. Swede found the money for the project, and Woods Hole Oceanographic Institution was chosen as the sub's home port. Allyn Vine's long-held dream would soon come true.

Trieste's two-person passenger compartment on the sub's underside had the same round shape as Beebe's bathysphere. On top was a gigantic tank that held 113,520 liters (30,000 gallons) of gasoline, used to help the sub rise at the end of a dive. (Gasoline was used because it is lighter than saltwater.) To sink, Trieste carried iron weights, which it left behind at the end of a dive.

Mauna Kea peak, Hawaii
4,208 meters (13,796 feet)

Mount Whitney,
Sierra Nevada Mountains
4,420 meters
(14,494 feet)

Mount Elbert,
Rocky Mountains
4,402 meters
(14,433 feet)

Great Plains

NORTH AMERICA

conning Tower

emergency
safety
Releases

Pressure Hull
+ Crew

Hand operated
release

Arm

Sample
basket

Arm
+
Sample
Basket

B

Mercury Trim 1 to 3

ALVIN
Schematic
(Possible)

Sphere

DISC

CHARGING

Indicator JBox

JBox

Science
T Box

1

2

3

Spare

Lights (6)

Science (4)

Relays

Sol. Valves

Propulsion + Trim (5·6)

Propul Box

V B Relay (6)

V B Box

Power

Keep Primary circuits SIMPLE + CHECKABLE

Isolate Indicator + Alarm functions from Primary Systems (Eliminate interlocks) outside sphere

Wiring — singles or 3 cond. Cable ← heavy duty

Minimum wire size — 16 AWG ← maybe even #14

Marquet – Vine
4 Sept 65

BIRTH OF A NOBLE FRIEND

"SEA PUP VI is a *complete* undersea research system. . . . It will perform manual tasks while hovering at great depths or resting on the ocean floor."—General Mills Press Release, September 8, 1961

In rundown offices over an old drugstore in the tiny town of Woods Hole, Massachusetts, a group of scientists and engineers joined forces in the early 1960s. Calling their office the "Drugstore," they named themselves the Deep Submergence Group. Their goal was to create a plan for a research submersible to carry scientists down to the bottom of the ocean. The scientists on the team would decide what the submersible should be able to do. The engineers on the team would figure out how to build a sub that could do those things. Together they would find a company to design and build the submersible.

Allyn Vine was asked to join the Deep Submergence Group, but he decided to stay on the sidelines as a helpful advisor. "I am already working one-and-a-half full-time jobs," he said. He wanted to keep his mind free for new ideas. Still, he was very interested in seeing the sub come to life. He often stopped in at the Drugstore to offer suggestions.

The Navy and the Deep Submergence Group put their heads together to draw up a list of requirements the new sub would need. The deepest parts of the ocean are completely dark, and the weight of water there is crushing. The sub had to be able to operate under those conditions.

(above)
An early wooden model of Alvin.

(left top)
Allyn Vine contributed ideas to Alvin's design. One was this sketch of a quick way to release the sub's passenger sphere in an emergency. (Fortunately, the quick release device has never been used.)

(left bottom)
Allyn also worked with the Alvin Group to make sure important design principles were remembered, as in his note on the sketch that reads "Keep Primary circuits SIMPLE + CHECKABLE."

Scuba Diver
90 m
(295 ft)
9 atmospheres

Sperm Whale
600 m
(1,968 ft)
60 atmospheres

Beebe's Bathysphere
922 m
(3,025 ft)
92 atmospheres

Alvin (1964)
1,829 m
(6,000 ft)
182 atmospheres

Trieste
10,900 m
(35,760 ft)
1,090 atmospheres

Note: objects not drawn to scale

The Weight of Water

One problem a submersible designer faces is creating a vessel that won't collapse under the weight of seawater. Though you may not be aware of it, the air around you has weight. To be exact, it weighs 1.03 kilograms per square centimeter (14.7 pounds per square inch). The weight creates an air pressure in all directions called "one atmosphere." The pressure of water is also measured in atmospheres. Since water is much heavier than air, the weight and pressure increases quickly with depth. With each 10 meters (33 feet) of depth, another atmosphere is added. So, a diver 20 meters (66 feet) under the surface is said to be diving at "two atmospheres."

But breathing air under pressure from a SCUBA tank becomes more dangerous as the diver goes deeper, and divers don't go much below 60 m (about 200 ft). To go deeper, people must travel in submersibles with walls strong enough to resist the pressure of the surrounding seawater. Inside these submersibles, pressure is the same as on the surface—one atmosphere. To dive to 10,900 m, Trieste had to be able to resist pressure greater than 1,100 kilograms per square centimeter (about 16,000 lbs per square in.).

It would be important for the sub to sink, rise, and move under its own battery power without being attached to a surface ship. It also needed to be neutrally buoyant. That means the sub's weight needed to be the same as the weight of the water it displaced, or moved out of the way. A neutrally buoyant sub can hang underwater in one place forever without using power. The sub needed to have as many windows as safely possible and a mechanical hand to collect samples. Finally, the sub needed to carry cameras that could be operated from inside, so passengers could record what they saw.

Once the list of requirements was finished, the U.S. Navy and the Deep Submergence Group looked for a manufacturer to make the sub. They asked several different companies to submit ideas that would meet their requirements. The design that was selected was created by General Mills engineer Howard "Bud" Froelich. The General Mills Company, in Minneapolis, Minnesota, makes ready-to-eat products.

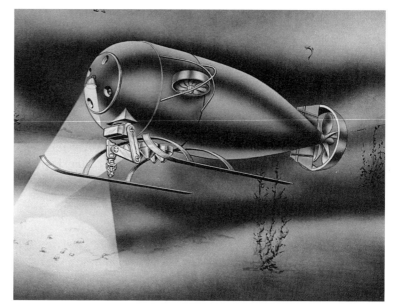

This is an artist's drawing of Bud Froelich's original design for *Sea Pup*.

Bud's design called for a fairly small vehicle—about as high and as long as a small pickup truck. A sub that size would be fairly easy to carry out to sea. The sub would have a mechanical arm and would be able to move up, down, forward, and backward under battery power. Designed to hover just above the ocean floor or to land there on skis, the sub could take two passengers for a period of 8 to 12 hours to a depth of 1,829 meters (6,000 feet). He called it *Sea Pup*.

The sub looked like it would be a great tool for exploring the deep ocean. There was just one problem. To the Deep Submergence Group the name *Sea Pup* just didn't sound dignified. They decided to change the name. After all, they were the ones who were going to operate it. No one remembers for sure who put the drawing of Alvin, the cartoon chipmunk, on the Drugstore bulletin board. But everybody agreed that the name, and even the picture, reminded them a lot of the man who had hoped for such a sub for so many years— Allyn Vine. Some people argued that the name *Alvin* was hardly more dignified than *Sea Pup*. Navy officials and even some WHOI officials were a little uncomfortable

Allyn Vine always insisted that the submersible was named for the cartoon chipmunk, not for him.

© Bagdasarian Productions

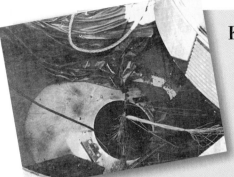

Ka-boom!

Parts of *Alvin* were built all around the country. Probably the most important part was the passenger sphere, which was built in Houston, Texas. Taking no chances, the Navy ordered three identical spheres. The most nearly perfect sphere of the three would be tested under pressure equal to that at 2,300 meters (7,500 feet) below the surface in a special pressure chamber, like a gigantic pressure cooker. The second best would be a spare. The third sphere would be put under increasing pressure until it collapsed.

The best sphere passed the 2,300-meters test. In February 1964, the third-best sphere went into the pressure chamber for the collapse test. The weld (a seam holding the halves of the sphere together) held at pressure equivalent to a depth of 2,300 meters...2,400 meters...2,700 meters. Finally, at pressure equivalent to 2,949 meters, the 18,160-kilogram (40,000-pound) lid of the testing chamber blew off with a tremendous blast.

Luckily, nobody was hurt. When the test observers looked inside, they found that the sphere was completely unharmed. It had proved stronger than the device built to test it!

Alvin's first passenger sphere was made out of a kind of steel called HY 100. Three spheres were made. All were tested to see which was the most nearly perfect.

The best of the three spheres is being lowered into the hull of the sub shell.

The sphere has been tested, polished, and painted and is in place in the base of the sub. Now the top and sail are fitted into position.

about the idea of giving their sophisticated new piece of equipment such a silly name. But then somebody looked at a dictionary and found that the original meaning of *Alvin* was "Noble Friend." Very dignified. The name *Alvin* stuck, and the Drugstore crowd started calling themselves the Alvin Group, a name still used today.

Alvin's first dive took place on June 26, 1964, off the dock at WHOI. Bud Froelich joined in the eighth dive. Allyn Vine was the passenger on the fourteenth dive. Inside *Alvin*, he and pilot Mac McCamis sank down 10 meters (about 35 feet) into the muck at the bottom of Woods Hole Harbor. The two men shook hands. "We did it."

Alvin as it looked when it was first launched in 1964.

Alvin Inside & Out

This is *Alvin* as it looks today. The shape of the sub is basically the same as it was in 1964. But now the sail, the "tunnel" on top of the sub, is red, not white. And the sub now carries much more sophisticated equipment.

Alvin is a little more than 7 meters long (about 23 feet) and 3.5 meters high (about 12 feet). It weighs about 7,800 kilograms (34,000 pounds), and can safely descend to a depth of 4,500 meters (14,764 feet). Its normal speed is 0.5 knots, but it can move at up to 2 knots (on land, that's about as fast as you normally walk).

Though the usual dive lasts 6 to 8 hours, *Alvin* carries equipment to support three people for 216 hours in case of an emergency.

This is an underwater telephone. Contact with the surface is very important for both safety and research.

Pilot and passengers enter *Alvin* through a hatch in the top, called the sail.

The rope used to lower *Alvin* to the water loops around a T-bar.

Samples are placed in these baskets.

Alvin has two manipulator arms, one on each side.

These iron bars make *Alvin* heavy enough to sink. To rise, the bars are dropped.

These switches control the lights outside *Alvin*. The lights are usually kept off until needed to save battery power.

The viewports are tiny. They have to be small to be strong enough to withstand the pressure of a deep-sea dive.

The pilot, Dudley Foster, controls the movement of the sub with a joystick.

This tiny sideport is being used by chemist Meg Tivey, who is interested in the water around the tube worms in the photograph on the right.

3

FIRST ADVENTURES

"Alvin proved that a deep submersible could do the most difficult job, retrieving not only an extremely dangerous weapon but also the nation's honor."—Mac McCamis, Alvin pilot

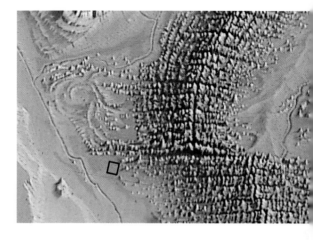

(above)
In 1966, Alvin was carried out to sea off the coast of Palomares, Spain, to recover a lost hydrogen bomb.

(left)
Those who dove with *Alvin* during the sub's first years had the questionable pleasure of sailing on *Lulu*, *Alvin's* first mother ship. Life on *Lulu*, named for Allyn Vine's mother, was rough but lively. She was crowded, leaky, and prone to break down. Still, cruises on *Lulu* were filled with the spirit of adventure that has always surrounded Alvin. Alvin was launched from the hole in the middle of *Lulu*.

lvin's looks sometimes surprise people. Blunt-nosed, stubby, and bright white, it doesn't look like a complex tool. "When people see [*Alvin*] for the first time, they're sort of let down," said George "Brody" Broderson, *Alvin*'s chief mechanic for many years. "They have this feeling it should be a long black sleek thing. Instead, they see what looks like a big white toilet and they ask, 'Is this the submarine?'"

Alvin wasn't always reliable during its first years. Its one-of-a-kind features were sometimes broken. *Alvin*'s mechanical arm didn't work well at first either. At times it didn't work at all. The electrical system sometimes quit. But the Alvin Group soon became experts at finding solutions when things went wrong. They were sure they could solve any and all problems. Now all *Alvin* needed was a chance to prove what it could do.

That chance came in February 1966. A hydrogen bomb weighing 5.8 metric tons (12,800 pounds) was accidentally lost at sea near Palomares, Spain, following an airplane crash.

The bomb was not live, so it would not explode. Still, the Navy wanted to find their top-secret weapon before any enemies did, and before the people of Spain became

19

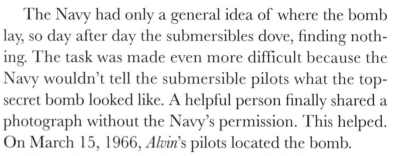

Easy Does It

Mac McCamis was one of the three *Alvin* pilots who worked in the recovery of the H-bomb. Here's how he described what it was like to free the bomb from the parachute: "With our meat hook in *Alvin*'s 'hand,' we started pulling the shrouds [the lines that attached the bomb to its parachute] and flaking [stretching] the 'chute down the slope. Things went well; it looked like we might finally unravel our ball of string.

After hooking a shroud, we would back down the slope, making sure the 'chute was lying flat so we wouldn't get entangled in it. Then I found that the 'chute wasn't completely out of its compartment on the bomb. So I pointed the hook into the compartment and tugged on a bunch of shrouds. Nothing happened...except *Alvin* was pulled right onto a 20-megaton hydrogen bomb. I tried again, this time fishing out one shroud. I was able to pull it some distance. Slowly, we were getting the job done."

angry and upset. So the Navy gathered 25 ships, 3,000 people, and several submersibles to try to find the bomb. *Alvin,* still brand-new, was invited along. The Alvin Group saw a chance to prove the value of their sub and promised to find the bomb.

The Navy had only a general idea of where the bomb lay, so day after day the submersibles dove, finding nothing. The task was made even more difficult because the Navy wouldn't tell the submersible pilots what the top-secret bomb looked like. A helpful person finally shared a photograph without the Navy's permission. This helped. On March 15, 1966, *Alvin*'s pilots located the bomb.

Next, the bomb had to be untangled from its huge emergency parachute. *Alvin* was selected for the job.

Clutching a giant hook, like the ones butchers use, in its robot hand, *Alvin* dove again and again. Hovering above the bomb, the pilots delicately worked the clumsy tool.

Finally, after 34 dives and a total of 228 hours on the seafloor, *Alvin* was able to free the bomb so it could be hauled to the surface by a Navy submarine.

But hydrogen bombs that need rescuing don't come along every day. The Alvin Group had to convince scientists to change the way they studied the deep ocean.

This is the bomb wrapped in its parachute. If the bomb could have exploded, it would have caused a blast larger than those at Hiroshima and Nagasaki at the end of World War II.

When *Alvin* traveled to sea with *Lulu*, the sub rode in an open space between the ship's two hulls. *Alvin* was lowered into the water on wire cables attached to a platform.

Instead of relying on tools sent down from the surface, scientists would have to start thinking of the deep ocean as a place they could actually visit.

Today, a scientist may wait years for a chance to dive in *Alvin*. But when the sub was first built, not many scientists were eager to get inside. Even though rides were free, *Alvin* was considered too unreliable.

Those few adventurous scientists who were willing to join *Alvin*'s early dives were rewarded many times over. "There are so many things to see…that is all that matters; you finally have no fear," remembered biologist Howard Sanders. "I felt like I was in the middle of the Milky Way. The exciting thing was when you would go down in the submarine, you would be where no one had been."

The good news about *Alvin* had just begun to spread when disaster struck. On October 16, 1968, two passengers and a pilot were preparing for a dive, *Alvin*'s 307th. The seas were rough that day. The three had a tough time climbing into the sub. They had just gotten in when a wire cable connecting *Lulu* to the "elevator" platform that supported *Alvin* for the launch and recovery snapped. Had the hatch, an opening at the top of *Alvin*, been closed, the sub would have stayed bobbing on the surface. But the hatch was open. Seawater flooded in and *Alvin* sank in less than a minute.

Fortunately, the three passengers made it to safety. Pilot Ed Bland, who escaped with only a sprained ankle, said, "I believe that the crew on the *Lulu*, holding on to the retaining lines as long as they did, gave us time to escape." *Alvin* wasn't so lucky. It sank without a trace.

A search effort was launched. But winter was approaching, and there wasn't much hope. It was like setting out at night to find a needle in the world's largest haystack. There was much discussion about whether it was even worth trying to find *Alvin*. After all, in those days the space program used each spaceship just once before abandoning it.

The members of the Alvin Group felt differently. They had worked hard on *Alvin*, repairing it over and over. They believed it still had a bright future. Fortunately, several high-ranking officials agreed. The following spring, the search was resumed. Days turned into weeks with no success. Then, finally, on June 14, 1969, it happened. A deep-towed underwater camera captured a picture of *Alvin*.

Alvin is found! The first sight of the long-lost Alvin, photographed by an underwater camera on June 14, 1969.

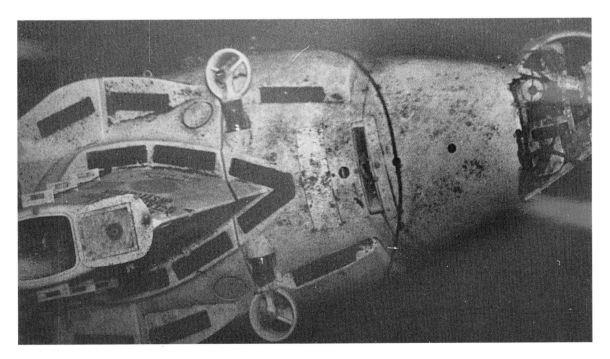

Alvin is just beginning its trip back to the surface after almost a year on the ocean floor.

It was a thrilling moment," said Alvin Group member Skip Marquet. "Especially after all that wild speculation about whether we'd ever find it. And there it was, pretty as you please."

Bringing *Alvin* back up to the surface took some doing. At last, on September 1, 1969, it was done. The sub was an absolute wreck. But the Alvin Group towed it back to Woods Hole and immediately began rebuilding their ruined "Noble Friend."

The *Alvin* Lunch

When *Alvin* was recovered after eleven months on the seafloor, an amazing discovery was made. Researchers found that a bag of lunch that had been placed inside the sub just before the passengers climbed in was still there. Inside the bag were three baloney sandwiches and three apples. After eleven months on the seafloor, the food was still fresh.

Biologists at WHOI immediately began to study the sandwich to find out how this could have happened. Most food is normally covered with bacteria. Food spoils when the bacteria begin to grow. From the "Alvin lunch," scientists learned that bacteria grow more slowly on the deep seafloor than on the surface—as much as one hundred times more slowly. This discovery led to many experiments and many more discoveries in the years that followed.

Alvin is finally rescued. You can see the chains from the crane that pulled *Alvin* to the surface.

4

HIGH PRESSURE, HIGH STAKES

"We went and we did it. It was a real gamble, and we knew that if we didn't bring it off, we would definitely go out of business."—Barrie Walden, WHOI Manager of Submersible Operations

By 1971, *Alvin* was as good as new. But its future looked bleak. The Navy told the Alvin Group they would have to begin to charge their passengers. *Charge them?* It was hard enough to get scientists to dive for free! They had to find a way to get the sub in an expedition that would attract scientists' attention.

Bob Ballard, a Navy man turned oceanographer, was hired to find missions for *Alvin*. He came up with a big project that would be difficult to do. But if it succeeded, it would bring *Alvin* the respect and recognition it deserved.

Bob knew of an important research expedition scheduled for the summers of 1972, 1973, and 1974. Called Project F.A.M.O.U.S. (short for French-American Mid-Ocean Undersea Study), the expedition would explore parts of a vast undersea mountain range called the Mid-Atlantic Ridge.

There was talk of including two French vessels, the submersible *Cyana* and the bathysphere *Archimède,* in the project. They would carry scientists down to explore a valley that ran down the center of the ridge. *Alvin,* more

(above)
How deep can it go? In the early 1970s, Alvin got ready to dive to new depths.

(left)
To get ready for the 1974 F.A.M.O.U.S. dives, scientists spent the summers of 1972 and 1973 towing underwater cameras back and forth over the dive site. The images were then laid out on the floor of a gymnasium, like a giant mosaic. Fuzzy and hard to read, these were still the best images then available. They were used to plan the dives made by Alvin, Cyana, and Archimède.

27

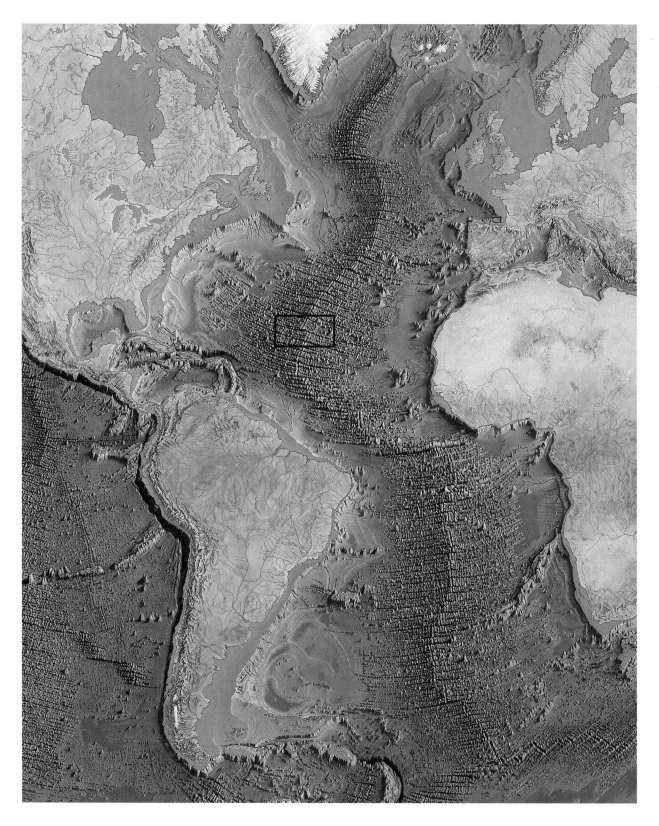

nimble than either of the French subs, would be perfect for the job. If *Alvin* performed well, the scientific community would surely begin to recognize the sub's value.

It was a good idea—a great idea, in fact. But there were two big problems. First, the valley lay at a depth of about 3,000 meters (10,000 feet). At that time, *Alvin* was only certified to dive to about 1,800 meters (6,000 feet). To enable *Alvin* to dive deeper safely, officials at WHOI decided a new sphere with thicker walls was necessary.

The Navy agreed to fund the work. A new type of metal called titanium might be the answer. It was lighter than the steel used to make the original *Alvin* passenger sphere. Therefore, it could dive deeper and still be light enough to be neutrally buoyant, that is, it would weigh the right amount to reach a certain depth and neither rise nor sink. But nobody had ever tried to build anything like *Alvin* using titanium. Would it work?

Even if the new material worked, there was an even bigger hurdle ahead. Some people thought it was an expensive gamble to bring *Alvin* along on the cruise. What if it didn't work properly? "What worthwhile science has ever come from a deep-diving submersible?" said one very experienced ocean scientist. He and his fellow scientists had "tried and true" methods for studying the deep sea. To make underwater maps, they used sonar, bouncing sounds off the seafloor and recording the amount of time it takes each sound to return. To study seafloor rocks, they scooped up samples. Why go down to the seafloor themselves? What would be the point?

Scientists who had dived in *Alvin* had an answer to these questions, the same answer given by those who dive in *Alvin* today. There is just no substitute for being in a place yourself and making choices about which objects or creatures to collect.

Bob Ballard worked very hard to convince the American scientists to bring *Alvin* along. It wasn't easy.

(left)
The Project F.A.M.O.U.S. dive site was on a portion of the Mid-Atlantic Ridge (see box on map). The Ridge is a seafloor mountain range that is larger and longer than the Rockies, Andes, and Himalayas combined. It is part of a much larger mountain range called the Mid-Ocean Ridge. Circling the globe like the stitches on a baseball, it is about 64,000 kilometers (40,000 miles) long. It is the single largest feature on our planet. The ridge is so big and so long that WHOI geologist James Heirtzler once said, "If it was painted red, you could probably see it from the moon."

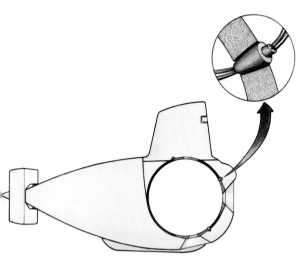

This cutaway drawing shows how each penetrator is tapered, like the top of a handmade candle. According to the design, the pressure of the deep sea should push the penetrators further and further into the sphere, making a seal that gets tighter as the sub dives.

But finally he got most to agree. He promised the sub would be ready on time. And he promised that having *Alvin* along on the mission would make it a huge success.

Here was another huge opportunity for *Alvin*. It was even more important than the chance to recover a lost bomb. But would *Alvin* be ready in time? Construction started right away, but it was a painfully slow process. The titanium was hard to work with and hard to weld. The sphere's schedule kept slipping farther and farther back. But the deadline for joining Project F.A.M.O.U.S. didn't change—June 1974.

The sphere was finally built and pressure-tested to 3,600 meters by the end of 1973. *Alvin* was almost ready. But a more challenging test lay ahead. Holes had to be drilled in the sphere for tubes called penetrators to carry electrical cables from *Alvin*'s outside instruments and video cameras to the inside. The penetrators were designed to be gripped tighter and tighter by the sphere as the sphere was squeezed by the weight of the ocean. The idea looked good on paper, but it had never been tried at this depth.

In early tests, it looked as if the penetrators would perform. But what if they failed? If one popped out, it would leave a hole in the passenger sphere that would cause *Alvin* to flood with seawater and kill all the people inside. The design was tested in the lab, but there was no way of being sure the penetrators would hold without going out to sea…and down to 3,000 meters. Time was running out. Only a few weeks remained before *Alvin* was to set off.

The Alvin Group took the sub out to the open ocean. Once there, *Alvin* went on a series of dives, each day a little deeper. Everything was fine at 1,000 meters…at 1,500 meters…2,000 meters…at 2,500 meters. But *Alvin* still hadn't dived to 3,000 meters.

On the last day, Barrie Walden, then a young engineer responsible for designing the penetrators, and the pilot sank deep beneath the waves for *Alvin*'s final test dive.

They stared at a set of motion-indicating dials that would tell them if the penetrators were about to blow out. "The thing that was scary about it is that the nuts on the necks of the penetrators were fairly strong," said Barrie. "So what we thought would happen, if anything, is that nothing would happen…nothing would happen . . . nothing would happen…and then suddenly PEEEEEEEEEW! The nut would fall out and the penetrator would be gone. It wasn't something you could think 'Well, I'll see it coming. And we'll go up.' It probably wasn't going to be that way."

Alvin descended. To 1,000 meters…2,000 meters… finally to 3,000 meters. *Alvin* hovered there long enough to be sure the penetrators were going to work.

Promising that *Alvin* would be able to take part in the F.A.M.O.U.S. expedition was a big risk. "We went and we did it," said Barrie. "We knew that if we didn't bring it off, we would definitely go out of business." The Alvin Group had done it again.

You're It!

Barrie Walden remembered the evening before the final test. "We had to get this 3,000-meter dive over with soon." As everyone went to bed, it hadn't been determined who would go on the dive. At dawn, one of the pilots wiggled Barrie's foot and said, "Get up." Barrie struggled up.

"Why?"

"Because you're going."

Barrie paused just an instant. "It should be just the same, whether it's you or one of your associates," he said later. "But it put things under a whole new light when I realized it was going to be me."

(above)
On deck for Alvin's test dive. From left to right: Allyn Vine, Larry Schumacher, Andy Eliason, Bob Ballard, and Barrie Walden.

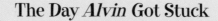

The Day *Alvin* Got Stuck

Geologists Bill Bryan of WHOI and Jim Moore of the United States Geological Survey were diving in *Alvin* as part of Project F.A.M.O.U.S., with Jack Donnelley as their pilot. The geologists were studying lava formations. They wanted to find a spot on the seafloor where the water temperature was a little warmer than usual. They thought they might find this warmer water in a fissure, a long, deep crack in the seafloor. So, they went looking for one. Unfortunately, it was just a little too narrow a space. The scientists' curiosity nearly cost them their lives.

Jack Donnelley had maneuvered *Alvin* about two meters down into the fissure. He held the sub in place as the scientists tried to take a temperature reading. As they waited for the temperature probe to make its reading, they realized something was wrong. *Alvin*'s port (left) and starboard (right) sides were both brushing up against the walls of the fissure. Jack tried to raise the sub up. It was no use. They were stuck.

"It was a really spooky feeling," remembered Bill Bryan later. "We would go up maybe half a meter and feel the sub bump against something. Jack tried everything, up, forward, back, and we hit something each time, not knowing what it was. It was as if somebody had put a big lid over us."

The story has a happy ending because both Bill Bryan and Jim Moore are very careful scientists. As *Alvin* traveled down into the fissure, they had noticed that the fissure's northern end was wider than its southern end. They thought *Alvin* might have been pushed into the narrower end by an ocean current.

It was a good hypothesis. Jack Donnelley tried moving *Alvin* backward, very slowly and very carefully. After two long hours, he was able to free the sub from its trap.

With *Alvin's* help, Project F.A.M.O.U.S. scientists were able to see ocean-floor formations firsthand and collect samples of volcanic rocks. They later broke these rocks apart and did experiments to figure out their age and what they were made of. From this, scientists were able to come up with theories about how and when the rocks were formed. Project F.A.M.O.U.S. was judged to be a spectacular success, and laid the groundwork for the study of deep-sea geology for the rest of the century.

As for *Alvin*, it was now able to dive deep enough to reach more than half of the ocean floor. The serious fun was about to begin.

Alvin was a big part of the success of the Project F.A.M.O.U.S. expedition. It made 17 dives, while Archimède and Cyana made a total of 27. Together the three subs recovered more than 1,300 kilograms (3,000 pounds) of rocks and samples, including these in the photograph above. (This is more than was brought back by all the astronauts who have visited the moon.) They also took 100,000 photographs.

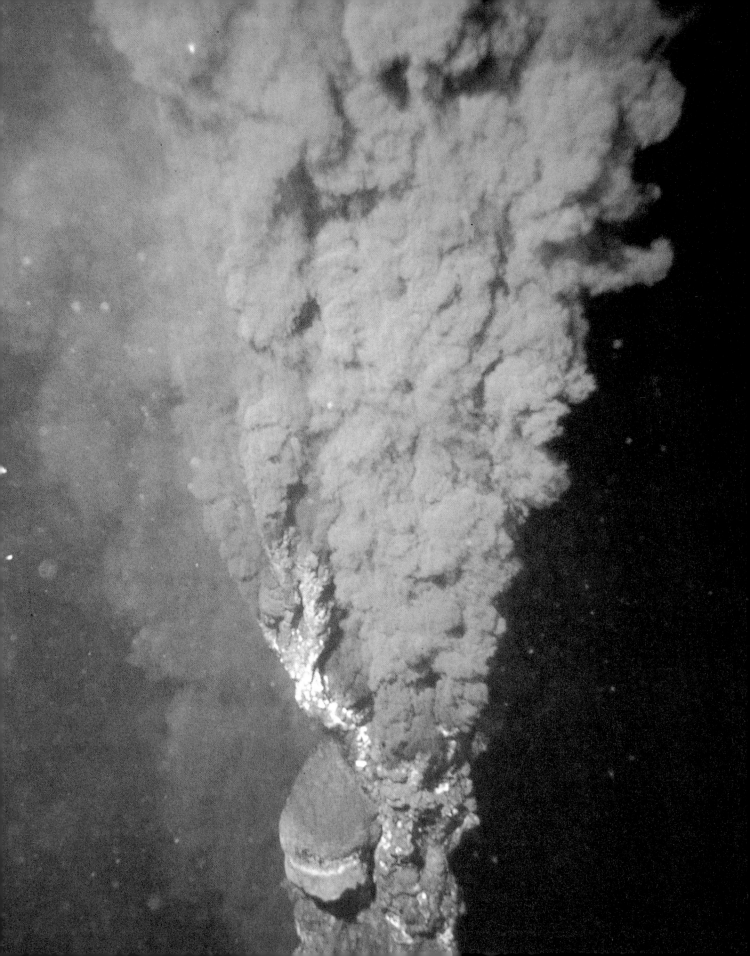

5

AN OASIS OF ALIENS

"I'd never seen a clam or a mussel that was a foot long. I said, 'This has got to be a dinosaur place.'"—Dudley Foster, *Alvin* pilot

Project F.A.M.O.U.S. caused scientists to start thinking differently about the deep ocean. They began to see the ocean as a place that could be studied in person. It was like the difference between studying the moon with a telescope and going there.

As so often happens with scientific discoveries, most of the answers brought back by Project F.A.M.O.U.S. raised new questions. Many of those questions were about pieces of volcanic rock covered with colorful streaks. (Most volcanic rock is pure black.) Scientists thought they might have been striped by a spray of chemicals and minerals. This "soup" could have come up from deep beneath the earth's crust, mixed with seawater, and then spewed up through geyserlike openings on the seafloor called hydrothermal vents. (*Hydrothermal* means "hot water.")

To prove this theory, scientists needed to find a vent. So, in 1977, *Alvin* began diving in the Pacific Ocean in an area near the Galápagos Islands off Ecuador. It was an active volcanic area, a likely place to find a hydrothermal vent.

(above)
Hydrothermal vents are home to some unusual creatures, such as these huge white clams.

(left)
This hydrothermal vent shape is called a chimney. Chimneys are often formed when minerals deposited around a vent opening pile up over time. The fluid shooting out of some chimneys is black, like the fluid from this chimney. Fluid in a "black smoker" can reach temperatures as high as 400°C (752°F).

Alvin's temperature probe, the striped pole at the left side of the photograph, reaches down to the seafloor, looking for warmer vent water.

The first dive of the cruise was to a place littered with clamshells. The place was nicknamed "Clambake." Scientists had found a slight temperature increase at this site, something that might indicate a hydrothermal vent. On February 17, 1977, geologists Tjeerd van Andel and John Corliss of the University of Oregon climbed into *Alvin* with pilot Jack Donnelley to "fly" down to Clambake. It was the 713th dive of *Alvin*'s career. For this dive, a heat sensor was attached to *Alvin*. It would beep each time the temperature rose one thousandth of a degree.

Just a few minutes after *Alvin* reached the seafloor, the sensor beeped. The sub's passengers peered out the windows, expecting to see the usual mud and rocks. Instead,

These white crabs are pretty much like crabs found elsewhere on the ocean floor. But these crabs get around without using their tiny eyes, since the world they live in is almost totally dark. When scientists spot a big group of them, they suspect that a hydrothermal vent is somewhere nearby.

This is a group of one kind of tube worms found at hydrothermal vents. Called *Riftia*, because they were found at deep-sea rifts, or cracks, they live in groups around the openings of hydrothermal vents. The water there is extremely hot and full of chemicals that would be poisonous to most living things. Their existence and how they survive have been the focus of many scientists' work since the tubeworms were discovered by Alvin divers.

they saw a seafloor oasis crowded with all kinds of bizarre animals. They were very surprised. Before that moment, most people had assumed that the deep seafloor was a desert with very little life.

Dudley Foster, an *Alvin* pilot since 1972, was one of the first people to see a hydrothermal vent. "I remember as a kid seeing these various sci-fi movies about lost valleys with dinosaurs. So when we first saw these oases . . . these huge giant clams and giant worms . . . it was incredible. You think you'd discovered some lost valley with dinosaurs. 'Cause they're big. Dinosaurs were big and these things are big."

Heading into the cruise, the hope had been to find a hydrothermal vent and collect rocks and water samples. Nobody expected to find odd animals, much less so many of them. It was an astounding discovery.

Two days later, John Corliss was diving again, this time with chemist John Edmond of the Massachusetts Institute of Technology. They headed back to Clambake. This time, they came across places where the seawater seemed to shimmer. The pilot used *Alvin*'s robot arm to collect jar after jar of water samples. And, to their growing astonishment, the reading on the temperature probe rose higher and higher. Not just one thousandth of a degree, but more than thirty degrees! What was going on here?

When the scientists returned to the ship, they opened one of the jars of water they had collected. A stench of rotten eggs filled the ship's lab, sending them all to the deck, gagging for fresh air. The water was full of a chemical that stank—hydrogen sulfide.

They were shocked! Seawater was supposed to be pretty much the same, no matter where it was collected.

Yet this water was loaded with hydrogen sulfide. The water of the deep sea was supposed to be almost the same temperature, almost everywhere. Yet this water was at least thirty degrees warmer than the water around it. The deep ocean was supposed to be almost deserted. Yet this place was full of strange creatures. How could these creatures live in darkness more than 3.2 kilometers (2 miles) down? What could they possibly eat that far away

When he learned of Alvin's great discovery, Allyn Vine was pleased and proud. He said, "It is wonderful that society let us build instruments to look at Mother Nature, and that when we got there, Mother Nature put on such a wonderful show."

from the sun? Was the warm, stinky seawater in some way providing food? What rules ran this strange universe?

Like the Project F.A.M.O.U.S. cruise before it, *Alvin*'s trip to hydrothermal vents had a huge impact on oceanographic research. The discovery of these vents and their fantastic communities of life has been one of the most important findings in biology, chemistry, and geology of this century. *Alvin* was once again at the center of a key oceanographic discovery.

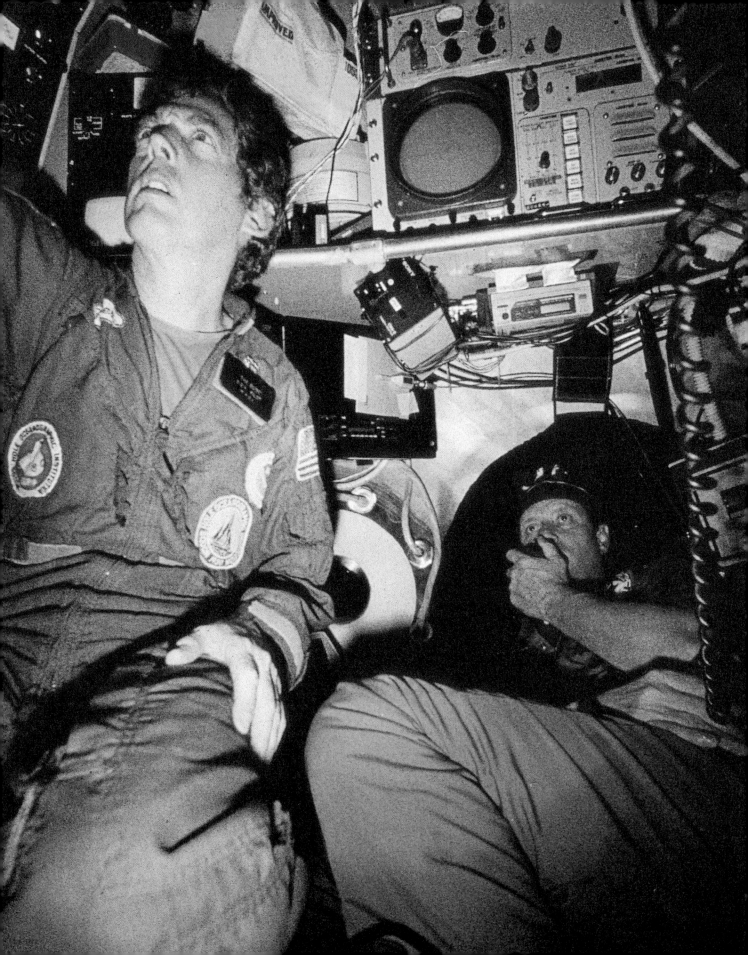

6

THERE HAS TO BE ANOTHER WAY

"Exploring the seafloor in Alvin is like being in the forest at night with a flashlight. There has to be a better way."—Bob Ballard

By the early 1980s, Bob Ballard, long one of Alvin's biggest champions, was rethinking deep-sea research. He was frustrated by Alvin's eight-hour dive time (the battery's limit), its three-passenger size, and its tiny viewports. Although *Alvin* was great to explore one place, it couldn't show "the big picture." "In 13 years [diving in *Alvin*] I had managed to explore a mere 40 miles of undersea mountain ranges," said Bob.

He wanted tools that could bring back more information, that could stay underwater longer, and that could let more people view a seafloor scene than just the three that could cram into *Alvin*. He imagined deep-sea sensors that would be operated by pilots who were far away, in a ship on the ocean surface, or even, someday, from a distant laboratory on dry land. The tools would capture video and still images. They would also use sonar to make pictures of underwater objects. They might use mechanical hands to collect samples.

If it were possible to build tools combining all these different abilities, Bob thought people might feel as if they were actually visiting these vast seafloor areas, even

(above)
Atlantis II, Alvin's mother ship from 1982 to 1996, carried ocean researchers to the sites of many discoveries.

(left)
Pilot Dudley Foster (left) and observer Bob Ballard hunt for a world-famous shipwreck in 1986.

41

The British luxury passenger liner *Titanic* sank on April 14–15, 1912, on its way to New York City from Southampton, England.

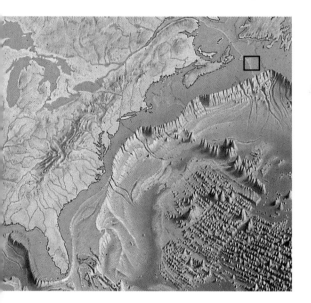

In the summers of 1985 and 1986, teams from WHOI traveled to a lonely spot off the coast of Newfoundland in search of the *Titanic*.

though they were viewing the scene from somewhere else. He called this sensation "telepresence."

The Navy's Office for Naval Research agreed that new tools were necessary, and they agreed to pay for their development. Bob gathered a group of topnotch engineers and researchers with experience in programming computers and building remote-control devices. The new group called itself the Deep Submergence Lab, or DSL.

The group quickly realized that the vision of what they wanted to create was ahead of its time. The biggest stumbling block they faced involved the cables they needed to power these new types of systems. At that time, if oceanographers wanted to collect underwater photographs, videos, or sonar, they would lower equipment to the site. The equipment would collect information and then be hauled back up to the surface where its film, videotape, or sonar record could be studied.

The DSL engineers wanted to figure out a way for pilots and scientists to be able to see what the devices were seeing while they were still underwater. That would let them make choices and decisions while the equipment was there to record the information. They also wanted to build robot-like devices called remotely operated vehicles, or ROVs, whose movements could be controlled by a distant pilot. Before these devices could be built, engineers needed powerful cables.

The best cable at the time was called coaxial cable, the cable that's used to carry cable television signals. It could carry enough electrical energy to power a single underwater black-and-white video camera and send its images back up to a monitor on a surface ship. Or it could carry enough energy to power an ROV directed by a pilot who was no more than a few hundred meters away.

The DSL knew there was a new type of cable being developed for use in telephone communications across oceans. Called fiber optic cable, it could carry enough electrical energy to power a group of underwater color video cameras or to control an ROV from miles away. But fiber optic cable was not fully developed in the early 1980s. So instead the DSL built the most powerful equipment they could using coaxial cable.

Jason Junior took part in many research cruises between 1986 and 1991. Unfortunately, *Jason Junior* was lost at sea while being transported to the Galápagos Islands.

The DSL built an underwater video camera system called *Argo*. It could send black-and-white video images made by a single camera from the deep sea up to the surface. They also worked to develop several versions of a simple ROV, finally making one they called *Jason Junior*. It could be operated by a pilot traveling inside *Alvin*, and could be sent off a few hundred meters from the sub to record video images in places where *Alvin* couldn't safely go.

It was time to put the new equipment to the test. And the group knew just where they wanted to go—to a place Bob Ballard had dreamed of visiting for many years—the graveyard of the ship *Titanic*.

The DSL hoped that if they could find the most famous shipwreck of all time, scientists around the world would hear about the tools they had built and would think of ways to use them in their own research. To find *Titanic*, the DSL joined forces with a French research group. Together they traveled to the area where the great ship had sunk.

The French group used a sonar device to begin the search. In three weeks of exploration, they were unable to find any trace of the ship. But they were also able to

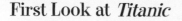

First Look at *Titanic*

In 1986, the group from WHOI's Deep Submergence Lab, along with members of the Alvin Group, explored the ruined ship. They dove in *Alvin*, equipped with *Jason Junior* (top right), the small remotely operated vehicle that carries a television camera. On the first dive, it seemed to pilots Ralph Hollis and Dudley Foster and to passenger Bob Ballard that everything that could break, did. The sonar system wasn't working. There was a leak in the battery pack. Though they knew where they wanted to go, the surface ship was unable to help *Alvin* keep track of its own position. They could have been close enough to the wreck to bump into it. But in the endless dark of the deep ocean, they might as well have been a hundred miles away.

Then, suddenly, everything clicked into place. The surface ship, *Atlantis II*, radioed: "Tracking is working. *Titanic* should be fifty yards to the east." Ralph, at the controls, turned *Alvin* toward the east. The three pressed their faces up against the viewports, straining to see. In a few moments, Ralph stopped. Before them, as Bob later wrote, was "an endless slab of black steel rising out of the bottom. *Titanic* was a few inches away. In that brief moment, we became the first ever to actually see *Titanic* in her grave." On later dives during the cruise, *Jason Junior* sent back dramatic and eerie images of the wreck of *Titanic*, such as this one (bottom right) of a ghostly chandelier.

About 160 pictures were put together to make this image of *Titanic's* bow section, the front half of the ship.

rule out many areas, so the group from the DSL had a smaller amount of seafloor to examine as they continued the search. The DSL used their video system, *Argo,* to conduct careful sweeps of the possible site of the shipwreck.

Argo made hour after hour of videotape. Every image was studied carefully by the people on the surface. At last, on September 1, 1985, in the very early hours of the morning, *Argo* made history. Cruising slowly across the area between ten to forty meters above the seafloor, it sent up images of a boiler, as well as coal, a telegraph, and the stern section of a large ocean liner. *Titanic* had been found.

It was an unforgettable discovery. And it more than proved its point—bringing new technology to the deep sea could lead to fascinating discoveries.

7

GETTING BETTER AND BETTER

"Progress gets made by people with different perspectives coming together."
—Dana Yoerger, research scientist

The successful voyages to *Titanic* helped prove that there was good reason to build the types of tools that the Deep Submergence Lab was inventing. But the group had a long way to go to achieve their vision of making tools to "visit" the seafloor without actually being there. First they had to build a much more powerful remotely operated vehicle than *Jason Junior*. Once fiber optic cable became available, this began to be possible. The DSL called their new tool *Jason*.

They equipped *Jason* with color video cameras, sonar, and even a mechanical hand like the one used on *Alvin*. First begun in the mid 1980s, changes to *Jason* are still underway today. The Deep Submergence Lab team is always looking for ways to improve *Jason*. They constantly keep an eye on new technologies, so that *Jason* can always be "state of the art." The vehicle has been taken apart and rebuilt over and over again as new technology becomes available. And the group is always looking for more scientists who want to use the special abilities that *Jason* can offer.

Even as *Jason* becomes more capable, like *Alvin* (or

(above)
Shipboard monitors like these show video images, sonar readings, and readouts from *Jason's* sensors. The sensors take measurements such as water temperature and salinity, or saltiness.

(left)
Jason at work in 1997, diving at an ancient Greek shipwreck off the island of Mykonos.

47

Jason and Medea

Jason now operates along with a video camera system called Medea that can take still and video images. Both are lowered overboard from a surface ship, which then moves very slowly over the area being studied.

Medea is attached to the ship by a steel-covered fiber optic cable. Jason is attached to Medea, and moves within a 50-meter (164-foot) circle under Medea.

surface ship

Medea

Jason

Jason Up Close

Jason is the size of a small car, weighing about 2,000 kg (4,000 lbs).

Emergency beacon If Jason became lost, this would help a ship find the sub.

Flotation module This offsets the weight of Jason's tools so the sub can stay neutrally buoyant.

Video camera

Thrusters These can move Jason up, down, and sideways with very delicate motions.

any piece of equipment), it has its limitations. Though it can stay underwater for days at a time, the people watching *Jason* work may be as much as ten city blocks away—straight up—in a ship's control room. From there, a pilot directs *Jason*'s movements. The pilot watches where *Jason* goes on video monitors. Crowding around the pilot are scientists, engineers, and technicians. They make decisions about where *Jason* should go and what it should do.

But they can only see what *Jason* "sees." And *Jason* can't navigate for itself. Every choice during a dive is made from the surface. Since *Jason* was built, technical equipment such as computers and video cameras have become much more sophisticated. These changes have allowed *Jason* to constantly improve its ability to "see" and navigate.

To help Jason "see" better, the DSL team is working on computer programs so that *Jason* can send a three-dimensional map of its position to monitors on the surface. That will help the people on the ship make better decisions about where to tell *Jason* to go and what to tell it to do.

It is also one of DSL's goals to find ways to improve *Jason*'s ability to travel along a predetermined route. After years of effort, *Jason* can now successfully travel a requested route or arrive at a deep-sea target with an accuracy that can be measured in centimeters.

Scientist Dana Yoerger is one of the people who design these improvements. Often, one of Dana's new ideas becomes a favorite feature, even though people resist it at first. Dana loves it when that happens, and thinks the different points of view are part of what makes his job fun. "[This] is an environment where you have . . . scientists and engineers [who invent devices], you have operations people [who are responsible for making sure the devices work every day], and then you have pilots and technicians,

(above)
"[Scientists are] very practical people," scientist Dana Yoerger of the DSL group says. "They say, 'I need a brighter light. I want a more reliable underwater connector.' Those are things we need to work on. But I want to make Jason into a supervised robot because it will work better. It will be able to do new things."

(below)
"There are always going to be times when the technology proves to be too much, or you push a little bit beyond what's reasonable," says Andy Bowen, Operations Manager for the Deep Submergence Lab. "We try to seek a balance between providing technological development while at the same time promoting meaningful results for research scientists."

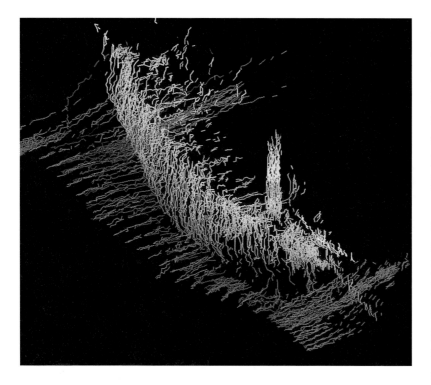

Using sonar equipment, Jason bounces sounds off of seafloor objects and then makes pictures of the shapes of the objects. In the early 1990s, Jason sent back detailed images of the wreck of the USS Scourge as it rested on the floor of Lake Ontario.

Ken Stewart led the group responsible for the development of Jason's sensors. "You can't control anything unless you've got the information you need to understand what's going on around you," says Ken.

real seadog types. . . . When we're looking at research problems to solve, we're not making problems up. We're trying to make underwater robots work better in ways our pilots like and that scientific users like."

Once improvements are successfully tested, they have to keep working properly, day in and day out. That's a challenge. But the group's focus has now moved from simply getting *Jason* to work to getting scientists to use it. That can be difficult, too. Scientists may have to wait years to get the chance to run a particular experiment. If the equipment fails, all that time has been wasted.

It's delivering results with *Jason* that gives the DSL group the biggest satisfaction of all. "Say you build a can opener," Andy Bowen says. "You could put it on a desk. But don't you want people to use it? So you go around opening up cans, and people use it and say, 'Well, that's a great can opener. That's cool. Can I get one? Can I use it?'" It's this kind of reaction that inspires the Deep Submergence Lab to keep improving *Jason*.

But vehicle development didn't stop with *Jason*. In the early 1990s, after working as a member of the Alvin Group for more than twenty years, Barrie Walden began to think about an entirely new type of research vehicle. Not one that was more complicated than *Alvin* or *Jason*—in fact, just the opposite.

He saw the need for a small, simple robot to do some of *Alvin*'s routine work. "If a device could be

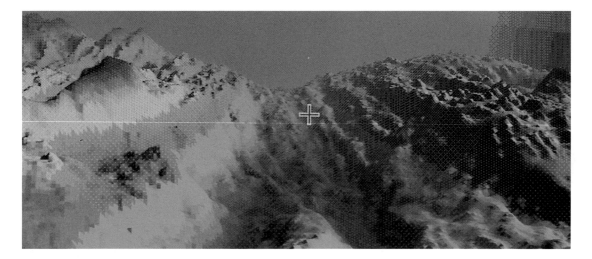

created that could stay in one place for a long period of time, much more information could be gathered at one spot, without the cost and complication of returning frequently in *Alvin* or another sub," he explained. Both *Jason* and *Alvin* need a ship nearby. The new device could be independent. That way, a ship could take it out, drop it off, then come back up to a year later to pick it up again.

To work, the vehicle would need to be able to find a particular spot underwater, follow a route, complete

(above)
Jason can gather information to make maps of the seafloor that appear to be in three dimensions, like this map of the Mid-Atlantic Ridge. It's interesting to compare this image with the series of pictures taken at the Mid-Atlantic Ridge during Project F.A.M.O.U.S. (page 26).

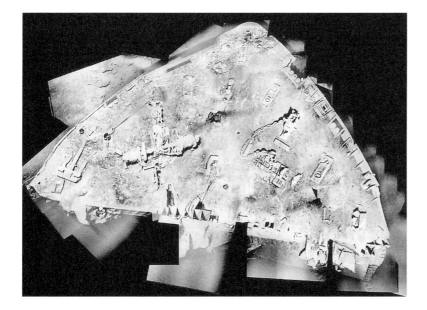

(left)
In 1997, Jason and Argo collected more than 137,000 images of the Derbyshire, a British ore carrier that sank off the coast of Japan in 1980. Images like this one of the 37-meter-wide (120-feet-wide) beam of the ship were used by investigators to help determine the cause of the wreck. This part of the wreckage was so large that the image had to be created by combining sixty separate photographs.

Al Bradley, one of ABE's inventors, holds a model of ABE built by a middle-school student. "The kid read about ABE in a magazine," said Al. "We think it really looks like ABE."

preprogrammed instructions (such as taking measurements), and do it day in and day out without any supervision. It would also need enough power to work for up to a year.

Barrie was trained in mechanical engineering. That means he understands how a device should be shaped, how its moving parts should work, and of what material it should be made. But to build the new vehicle, he needed people with other skills as well as his own.

He went to see Al Bradley, an engineer who has built many deep-sea research devices. Al knows electronics. He can build a system that is reliable and uses minimal power, which is very important if the device is to stay on the job for a year at a time.

Barrie's idea was to have *Alvin* place a beacon on the ocean floor. A beacon is a device that sends out sound pulses at regular intervals. The device he wanted Al to help him make would be able to find the beacon by "listening" for these sounds. The robot would use the beacon as its "home base" and from there go off on missions. It would return to the beacon at the end of each trip and go to "sleep"—turning off its power until its internal clock "woke" it up again.

Al liked Barrie's idea, and they divided the tasks. Barrie would build the vehicle's body and "muscles"—its flotation devices and instrument casings. Al would build its "nerves"—the systems that would operate the sub's motor, cameras, and sensors. They named their cool new tool "ABE"(short for "Autonomous Benthic Explorer").

Next, they needed somebody to program the vehicle's "brain"—a control system that could tell ABE to turn itself on and off, when and where to go, and when to make measurements and record observations. The right person for the job, they knew, was Dana Yoerger.

Working together, the three built the vehicle. They knew that it needed to be shaped so that it wouldn't tip over by accident. So they put flotation devices in two long tubes on top and ABE's "brain" on the bottom. They stood back and took a good look at the vehicle. It looked familiar. In fact, it looked like *Star Trek*'s *Starship Enterprise*! Though the similarity was an accident, they decided to have a little fun, and they painted *Enterprise*'s identification number, NCC1701/B, on ABE's starboard, or right, side.

You can't be too careful when launching a one-of-a-kind piece of gear. ABE is hoisted overboard by a crane, as three people make sure it doesn't bang up against the ship.

As with *Alvin* and *Jason* when they were first built, few scientists were eager to use the newly finished ABE for their research. But one scientist, WHOI geologist Maurice Tivey, was very excited by the new device. He liked the fact that ABE is small, lightweight, and easy to move. "It can go on any little ship, straightaway, and it can collect the data for us," said Maurice. Maurice agreed to be part of ABE's first dive.

The ABE team had talked with Maurice during ABE's development, so he was aware of what it probably could and could not do. But the only way to find out for sure was to go out to sea. Maurice wanted to use ABE to measure magnetism in rocks that had recently been created by a seafloor volcano. "I asked them if they could do it," said Maurice. "They said, 'Sure we can do it. Well . . . we've never actually done it, but we can do it.'"

Using ABE to collect the information was a risk. This would be ABE's first mission. Would it work? Maurice had a lot of faith in the technology and its designers. But just to be sure, he brought along some more tried-and-true equipment, too.

As it turned out, ABE performed perfectly, collecting even more information than Maurice had expected. ABE flew down to the seafloor and landed in the caldera, or hole in the middle, of the volcano Maurice wanted to study. ABE then climbed out of the caldera and surveyed a ten-kilometer square area of very rough ground.

Using data from ABE, Maurice was able to determine that the caldera where

Maurice Tivey made this picture to show the information collected by ABE during a survey of a seamount, or underwater mountain, off the coast of Oregon. The colors in the image indicate the amount of magnetism in the seamount's rocks. Rocks with the highest level of magnetism look orange. Rocks with the lowest level of magnetism look dark blue. Seamount heights are recorded as negative numbers, showing depth beneath the ocean surface.

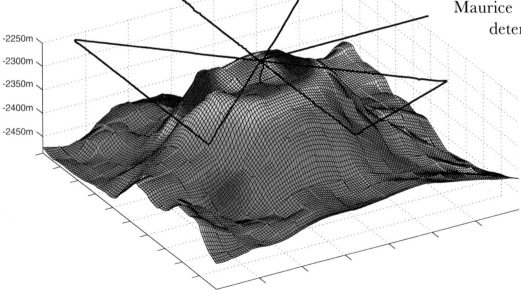

-2250m
-2300m
-2350m
-2400m
-2450m

the robot had landed was still hot—something none of them had known before ABE visited the spot. "Maurice taught us a very simple lesson about autonomous vehicles," Dana Yoerger remembered. "They are simple-minded, but when they work, they do what you tell them to do. Those capabilities really help scientists do their work."

All About ABE

ABE, short for Autonomous Benthic Explorer, is about 3 meters (10 feet) long, and about 1.5 meters (about 5 feet) high. It can operate at a depth of 6,000 meters (about 20,000 feet). Its battery power will let it operate for up to 100 hours over the course of a year.

Upper pods Each pod contains three glass balls for flotation.

Propellers

Lower housing This holds the batteries and electronics, such as a digital video camera and a magnometer to record the magnetic properties of the seafloor.

The lower housing also holds a device to measure the conductivity (which basically means the saltiness) and the temperature of seawater at different depths.

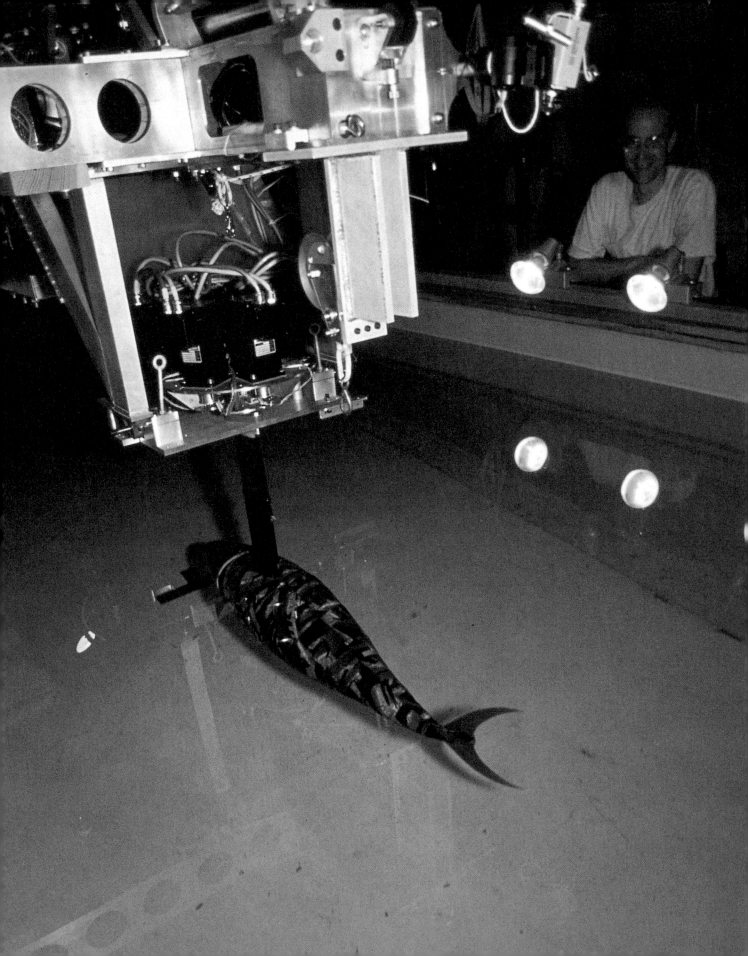

THE BEST TOOL FOR THE JOB

*"Technology has always been a problem for oceanographers.
It always has been, and it always will be."—Allyn Vine*

(above)
Researcher Lauren Mullineaux relies on information she gathers while traveling to the seafloor in *Alvin*.

(left)
In development at the Massachusetts Institute of Technology is "Charlie," a robot bluefin tuna that copies the motion of an actual fish. Charlie may point the way to creating low-power robot submersibles that can stay underwater for very long periods of time without needing to recharge their batteries.

Because humans are not capable of living underwater, technology will always be a major part of the study of the deep ocean. People have created tools to make this possible, each tool bringing new problems to light, which are in turn solved by later inventors. The process repeats itself over and over again. An innovator sees a better way to investigate the ocean. Others resist, saying that old ways are best. The innovator finally succeeds in convincing a few others. A prototype is built as people continue to doubt. A few risk takers try it. The prototype is debugged. As the first results come in, people begin to take the invention seriously. Then, finally, just as the "innovation" is accepted, a new inventor begins to see a better way to solve a problem, and the process starts over again.

Lauren Mullineaux, research scientist at WHOI, has studied the animals at hydrothermal vents for many years. She has made more than twenty dives in *Alvin*. For her, a submersible like *Alvin* will continue to be the best tool, at least for some of her experiments that require the delicate touch of *Alvin*'s mechanical hands. "The idea that submersibles that carry people are out of date has been around for a decade or more," she says. "But the

REMUS, short for Remote Environmental Monitoring UnitS, has been designed at WHOI to get information on coastal areas. At just 137 cm (54 inches), REMUS is small enough to carry in a car, or to be sent as baggage on an airplane. REMUS can travel to a series of underwater stations, collecting information about conditions at each station. The first REMUS unit is being used off the coast of New Jersey. A second REMUS will soon be put to work off the coast of Massachusetts.

demand is still very much there." *Alvin* continues to draw users, she believes, because "it's bugproof and bombproof, and that's what the scientists want."

Andy Bowen of the Deep Submergence Lab is excited to think about the discoveries that lie ahead using vehicles like *Jason*. He sees *Alvin* as a useful tool for collecting samples, whereas *Jason*, to him, is a way to take in all kinds of information about the seafloor. For example, before taking *Jason* to study a crack in the seafloor called a fault, a scientist might know that the fault is in a certain location and runs from north to east. But that's all he or she may know. After a few dives in *Jason*, it will be possible to determine the fault's location, how deep it goes, and how it relates to everything else around it.

Maurice Tivey is happy with the development of ABE, which is ideal for his purposes. For many years, he's worked with systems towed from ships on the surface. "It's a pain," he says. "You have to deal with the ship. The big, long cable has been one of my pet peeves for a long time. Being able to program ABE to go off and do its thing is great." He's even looking forward

to a time when devices like ABE can be monitored from shore. "That would be the best," he says. "Then I wouldn't get seasick. It would be nice to come into the lab and log on and say, 'Where are you today? Oh, great. I want you to go to this area.' That would be cool."

As time goes on, each type of vehicle will continue to evolve and improve in ways we can't even imagine today. And yet, no sooner will a vehicle's inventor pronounce it perfect than somebody else will shrug and say, "It's great, but I wish we had a vehicle that could . . ." and the process of invention begins all over again.

Phoning Home

Researchers at the Massachusetts Institute of Technology who are designing and building the deep-diving robot *Odyssey* are working hard on a new feature. It's a device similar to a cellular phone. *Odyssey* will use this "phone" to communicate with other vehicles and with scientists back in their laboratories.

It's possible that in the not-too-distant future, an *Odyssey* fleet will roam the seas, delivering information to and taking directions from their scientist bosses back on dry land.

GLOSSARY

ABE Short for Autonomous (can operate by itself) Benthic (ocean bottom) Explorer, a new robot submersible that someday may stay underwater for up to a year at a time.

Alvin A deep-diving research submersible that can carry three passengers on dives down to 4,000 meters (about 13,000 feet) for up to eight hours at a time.

Argo An underwater camera system towed from the surface by a research ship.

bacteria Single-celled organisms that often grow in large colonies, or groups.

bathysphere [BATH-i-sfear] A steel-walled, circular vessel used for deep-sea diving.

beacon An underwater transmitter that sends out sounds to help a submersible find its location.

caldera [kal-DARE-uh] A large circular depression at the top of a volcano.

chemist A scientist who studies the composition and properties of substances and how they change.

chimney A chimney-shaped structure built of minerals from a hydrothermal vent.

coaxial cable [koh-ACK-see-ul KAY-bul] A bundle of copper wires used to carry electrical impulses, especially video or television signals.

fiber optic cable Lightweight cable that uses very thin glass tubes to carry video signals.

fissure [FIZH ur] A long, deep crack in the seafloor.

geologist A scientist who studies the structure and history of Earth.

hydrogen sulfide [HI-druh-jen SUHL-fide] A chemical, poisonous to humans and to most living things on Earth, that comes from hydrothermal vents.

hydrothermal vents [HI-dro-THUR-mul vents] Cracks in the seafloor that let chemicals, such as hydrogen sulfide, and minerals come up into the ocean.

Jason A remotely operated vehicle controlled from the surface by a long cable.

Jason Junior An underwater camera used between 1986 and 1991 to make video images in the deep sea.

joystick A hand-operated device used to direct the movement of an object.

Marianas Trench The deepest trough in the ocean at 10,900 meters (35,800 feet).

mechanical engineering The invention, building, and repair of machines.

Medea [meh-DEE-ah] An underwater camera system towed from a surface ship. It is often connected to *Jason*.

Mid-Atlantic Ridge An underwater mountain range that is part of the Mid-Ocean Ridge.

Mid-Ocean Ridge A 67,000-kilometer-long (about 40,000 miles) global underwater mountain range.

minerals Solid substances found in nature that are not alive and are not formed from plant or animal matter.

neutrally buoyant [NEW-tral-lee BOY-unt] An object is neutrally buoyant when it weighs the same as the water it displaces and is suspended. A positively buoyant object weighs less than the weight of water it displaces and rises. A negatively buoyant object weighs more than the weight of water it displaces and sinks.

oasis A place of life in the middle of a desert.

oceanographer A scientist who studies the physical, chemical, biological, and geologic features of the ocean.

Odyssey [ODD-i-see] An autonomous vehicle with a device to communicate with scientists and other vehicles.

passenger sphere A steel ball in which passengers travel safely to deep-sea depths.

penetrator [PEN-uh-tray-tor] A tapered tube that carries electrical cables from *Alvin's* outside instruments and cameras to the inside.

pressure chamber A device designed to test the ability of an object to resist pressure.

REMUS Short for Remote Environmental Monitoring UnitS. This device collects information on coastal areas.

ROVs Short for Remotely Operated Vehicles, submersibles that carry no passengers and are connected to a surface ship by a tether.

salinity Amount of salt in the water.

sonar A device for detecting underwater objects by reflection of sound waves.

submersible An underwater vehicle, usually one used for scientific research. (A submarine usually refers to an underwater vehicle used for warfare).

titanium A very strong, lightweight metal.

Trieste [TREE-est] A submersible that operated in the late 1950s and early 1960s. It made the deepest underwater dive ever, to the Marianas Trench.

FURTHER READING

Ballard, Robert D. *Exploring the* Titanic. New York: Scholastic, 1988.

Dipper, Francis. *Mysteries of the Ocean Deep.* New York: Copper Beech Books, 1996.

Johnson, Rebecca L. *Diving into Darkness: A Submersible Explores the Sea.* Chicago: Lerner, 1989.

Kaharl, Victoria A. *Water Baby: The Story of* Alvin. New York: Oxford University Press, 1990.

Kovacs, Deborah and Kate Madin. *Beneath Blue Waters: Meetings with Remarkable Deep-Sea Creatures.* New York: Viking, 1996.

Markle, Sandra. *Pioneering Ocean Depths.* New York: Atheneum, 1995.

Massa, Renate. *Ocean Environments.* Austin, TX: Raintree Steck-Vaughn, 1998.

Van Dover, Cindy Lee. *Octopus' Garden.* New York: McGraw-Hill, 1997.